T0090597

Here,
Now

Here, Now

Cinnamon H. Lofton

Loving Life Foundation
Seattle, Washington

Order this book online at www.trafford.com
or email orders@trafford.com

Most Trafford titles are also available at major online book retailers.

© Copyright 2009 Loving Life Foundation.
All rights reserved. No part of this publication may be reproduced, stored in a retrieval system, or transmitted, in any form or by any means, electronic, mechanical, photocopying, recording, or otherwise, without the written prior permission of the author.

Printed in Victoria, BC, Canada.

ISBN: 978-1-4269-1732-5 (sc)
ISBN: 978-1-4269-1-733-2 (dj)

Library of Congress Control Number: 2009939246

Our mission is to efficiently provide the world's finest, most comprehensive book publishing service, enabling every author to experience success. To find out how to publish your book, your way, and have it available worldwide, visit us online at www.trafford.com

Trafford rev. 11/16/2009

 www.trafford.com

North America & international
toll-free: 1 888 232 4444 (USA & Canada)
phone: 250 383 6864 ♦ fax: 812 355 4082

Loving Life Foundation
cinnlofton@gmail.com
phone: 206 303 7602   fax: 206 402 4441

I dedicate this book to the memory of my first spiritual teacher and mentor, Ken Keyes, Jr. He introduced me to Living Love and, ultimately, to myself, my "big" self. Ken shares this dedication with the memory of my second and greatest teacher, my late husband, Donald E. Lofton. My love continues to pour out to them both.

INTRODUCTION

As I begin to write the introduction to what for me has been a life's journey, the first words that spring from my heart are thank you. Thank you to God for the life I've been blessed to live. Thank you to the biological children who bravely chose to enter life through me and allow me the extraordinary joy of being their mom. My heart says thank you for all the non-biological children who were born of my heart, not my body, who do me the honor of thinking of me as Mom, or "Cinnamom," as they often refer to me.

I would love to list the names of every person who ever inspired, moved, or motivated me in my life. Though I intend to spare you, the reader, that extensive list, I am nevertheless humbled by their number. You all know who you are; please know how grateful I am.

Sincere thanks goes to you the reader for being attracted to the title of this book. That you are willing to pick it up and spend your time experiencing yourself responding or even not responding to its message is a joy to me. Blessings to you and to all seekers.

I humbly thank Heidi Grant who has co-produced this work with me. She is my soul mate, my dearest heart. Her participation in my life as well as this book is immeasurable. Words cannot express my heartfelt gratitude.

My introduction to Living Love, the path of my mentor, Ken Keyes, Jr., was through his *Handbook to Higher Consciousness*. I learned his Twelve Pathways to Higher Consciousness, which eventually helped me to be willing to expand my spiritual awareness. Consequently, my heart's knowing made it possible for me to take responsibility for sharing the pathways with the world according to my own spiritual awareness of them. This led me to reshape the format of Living Love as I've known it. *Here, Now* is neither steeped in doctrine or historical perspective. It lives according to its own name, emerging from a simply grateful heart, present and being.

My work is not about religion. It couldn't be further removed from the institution known as religion. It is about God. Every breath I breathe like every page of *Here, Now* is an act of love and devotion, inspired by our Creator. That's right, OUR Creator. Father/Mother God, Creator of us all. Every word of this book is written to honor and spread God's message in the world: God is Love; Love is all that matters. Everything else can be attributed to mind games which keep people stuck in their illusions of separateness. Love is the healer, the answer. It is the one truth.

I offer up this work to you to help you grow in the spirit of oneness. Through these pages, I am here, supporting you in making the choice to experience more love and respect for yourself. May you be inspired to know that you are a member of the sacred family of man, inclusive of all people and their cultures.

World peace is achieved one heart at a time. Join me in creating that peace, here, now.

Lovingly,

Cinnamon H. Lofton

This book may be way too simple for you.

(I'm not kidding.)

Or you may recognize it

as a powerful guide for joy.

God is co-author of this book.

If you don't believe that, put it down right now.

If God wasn't the co-author, there would be no book and there would be no you to put it down.

If you believe you're "only human," and are not willing to budge....you're thumbing your nose at enlightenment.

Nothing is more important
than enlightenment.

Not romance,

not money,

not parenthood.

Nothing.

This book could be summed up in two words:

Live Love.

Peace is not a state of mind. It is a state of being. There is no need to fight with your mind. Just simply breathe and step out of it.

Don't push down your feelings. Breathe and let them out. It's like taking out the trash. You wouldn't sift through the trash to see what's inside. It's trash!! Dump it or recycle it into something useful!! Either way, get it out of the house!

You can't think your way to higher consciousness, not with religion or meditative poses, yoga, or any thought process.

It's this simple:

Breathe in the love that is your birthright, exhale, and relax into it.

(If you are not free, you are still thinking.)

Simplicity.

Simplicity.

Simplicity.

The difference between thriving and surviving is found in the breath.

Breathe NOW.

Are you breathing yet?

Be still.

Close your eyes. Breathe deeply, and let the love that is in you surface. No matter who you are, love is there in you. Release it and know the joy of expressing it.

Do it now.

Choosing love is the key to wholeness because when you choose love you are automatically enrolled in service and in your own joy, in your own compassion. Once you choose love, you take the blinders and the limitations off. You see the innocence of yourself and others. Create a discipline of choosing love…

…and choosing love…

…and choosing love.

There's only one question:

What serves love here?

If you create the discipline to wake up in the morning and surrender to love, you continue to breathe that breath of love that you've been breathing all through the night in your sleep. There is no decision-making. There is just being.

Someone asked me how I could say that rape was not wrong. She went further to say that she couldn't believe that <u>anyone</u> would say rape is not wrong.

Having been raped in my life more than once, I could answer from an experiential rather than a philosophical perspective.

Rape is a fearful act of violence that perpetuates fear and violence. It does great harm both physically and psychologically. It is unacceptable behavior that requires addressing with a great deal of discipline.

Forgiveness is the key ingredient if one is to heal from the experience of rape.

That does not mean the rapist should simply walk away, undisciplined.

It does mean that if one does not forgive and heal, one will be forever chained to the experience and unable to know the joy of freedom, here and now.

Since here and now is all we have, why would you want to attach yourself to a right/wrong mindset that can only bring suffering and further unhappiness?

Are you willing to perceive your own innocence?

The greatest gift you can give *anyone* is to believe in their innocence.

You can only give what you've got.

When you are willing to distinguish the doer from the deed and see that love is the core of every person, forgiveness will become so natural that it will be yours in one simple breath. The inhale will be full of forgiveness and the exhale will contain the realization that the doer is innocent, that there is actually nothing to forgive.

The only way to see the innocence in ALL people is to decide to trust in the spiritual nature of life. There is no hardship, no calamity that is without spiritual purpose. Every so-called "evil" provides an opportunity for the love inside of us to demonstrate its power and its invincibility. Every person that is in fear gives us the opportunity to love the 'unlovable.' Every challenge allows us to show ourselves how big we are.

You will NEVER get from life more than you can handle.

When you make this truth your own, you will stop fearing the future based on your past experiences. Life will become fully here and now, unadulterated, playful.

You are used to being scared. You've been trained since childhood to be scared, taught by your parents that the way to be safe from danger is to be afraid of it. You can train a child not to walk into traffic with intelligent information about it. Scaring them with thought of death or injury is not necessary.

Often when you are taking offense to what someone said, if you go within, you will usually find that there is in it a grain of truth, a truth that you are resisting. Explore this courageously and you will find insight.

Whenever someone accuses you of a perceived wrong-doing, whether you've actually done the deed or not, your freedom lies in simply asking them to forgive you.

Love

Discipline

Forgiveness

How do you depersonalize people's treatment of you? Realize that people can only give you what they've got. If a person has filled himself up with disrespect for years, how's he going to give you respect? It's not about you. So step aside. Learn the art of spiritual aikido instead.

STEP ASIDE!!!

Grief is like bath water. When you first get in, it is really hot. When you relax and sit with it, it becomes a comfort and a cleansing. When it cools down, it's time to get out.

Without the connection of body, mind, and spirit, there can be no oneness.

So, how do you make that connection?

Be aware of when you are not feeling whole and peaceful and say, 'Yes.'

"Yes, I will allow myself to be connected to the sacredness of the body I've chosen, the mind that helps me manage that body, and the spirit that makes it all worth it."

Now, allow yourself to KNOW this experience from the inside.

Breathe in and be it.

Whether or not you are willing to say yes is not what makes you loveable. Being willing to say yes simply allows you to enjoy the truth that you are loveable.

Doubting your own doubt is a turning point.

To continually ask "WHY?" is to constantly resist taking full responsibility for what you're creating in your life. ("Why me?" "Why now?" "Why….?" "Why…?")

Replace the word 'WHY' with 'YES.' There's power in yes. Yes says, "I see. I can deal with this 'what-is.'" Yes!!

Instead of Why….say Wow!!

Instead of Why….say Oh!!

Instead of Why….say THANK YOU!!

"Yes."

(Keep practicing.)

We spend so much more time feeding ourselves nutritionally than we do feeding ourselves spiritually.

When you accept life on its terms, you step through the pain barrier and know peace.

Peace is found in the eye of the storm.

Be courageous.

It's not about what you do. It's *all* about where you are coming from that counts.

Let this book become a roadmap to your heart. The answers are all inside you. The tendency is to look "out <u>there</u>" for the answers.

The answers are just <u>not</u> outside yourself.

Why then, says your mind, am I reading this book? Good question. <u>Very</u> good question. You're reading this book because your mind is programmed to believe that the answers are in books or with someone or something outside yourself.

At the same time, your spirit also brought you to this book because you have reached a point in your human journey that is giving you the opportunity to trust your own awareness. You can now start searching the inner knowings of your heart.

The answers that will lead you to the experience of joy and peace are beyond the human mind's understanding.

There is a vast difference between knowing something as an observation and holding on to it as a judgment.

A judgment keeps you separate and heavy and fearful of the future. There will usually be an emotional charge with it, often involving superiority or righteousness.

An observation is a tool that you use to be here and now with your decision-making. It is an assessment of what seems to be so, often triggering your compassion and desire to assist, comfort, or applaud.

It's amazing how people are willing to rise to your trust when you are willing to put it out there.

Change requires change.

Too simple? Here's the "how to."

Make a list of everything in your life you'd like to be different.

Beside each statement, write exactly what you'd be willing to do to achieve that change.

It is likely that what shows up is what you're <u>not</u> willing to do to achieve the changes.

Sit with that unwillingness. See how you feel about it. Notice if you're judging yourself. If you are...

STOP THAT!

YOU'RE <u>INNOCENT</u>.

Don't wallow around in the dirt, saying, "I fell down! I fell down!" Get up! Just look at getting up. That is all that matters.

GET UP!

Learn the difference between an observation and a judgment and you've found one of the keys to peace and joy.

How busy we are probing other people's lives, finding all the ways they could change and be "better."

Mirror, mirror, on the wall...

The heart mind says,

"Totally trust that love works."

The intellectual mind says,

"Well, maybe…..but….."

If you're not willing to get your 'but' out of the way,

you're thumbing your nose at enlightenment.

Get that 'but' out of the way!

You are safe because you choose to believe that you are safe and for no other reason.

One of the grand contradictions in life is that there are no rules. There are no rules and yet one of the rules happens to be:

"When in doubt, DON'T."

The mind is the architect of doubt. It will get on one shoulder and say, "Yes," then immediately be on the other shoulder saying, "No."

If you want to be sure you are making spiritually sound decisions, make them from your heart-mind.

Most people continually choose their beliefs (which are a product of the mind) over what they know (which comes from the heart).

We're taught from childhood to stay in "your right mind," which usually refers to the intellectual mind. Yet what we *think* is so often in conflict with what we *know* in our hearts. I would rather *know* from my heart than to *think* that I know.

The mind is the author of confusion.

Quick!

Get out of your mind.

If you let your life be controlled by your untrained intellectual mind, you'll be on a constant emotional roller coaster.

If you are willing to train your intellectual mind to be the servant of your heart mind, you'll be like a reliable smooth-sailing ship, strong enough to weather the waves and storms of life with little or no real damage.

The spiritually untrained intellectual mind is the servant of fear. The spiritually trained mind is the servant of Love.

The question begs: Why would you choose to serve a tyrant (fear) when you could serve Love and be free of the chains to which fear binds you?

Stop reading now and think about it.

If we are not in a space of loving when we leave any relationship, we take all that unhappiness with us. Your mind says, "If I leave, then I'll get some fresh air. It will give me a break."

It won't.

Are you willing to create a whole new dialogue and memorize it word perfect?

A dialogue of Love?

Truth is not far away. It is not hidden.
It is planted deep in the center of your heart.

If you haven't uncovered it yet, dig deeper.

Be courageous enough to be yourself, to follow God's guidance even when it completely contradicts what the world has dictated is the RIGHT way to be.

So many people believe that anger can be constructive. They believe this because they think that anger is the best, if not the only, means of accessing their courage.

Thinking gets them into trouble.

Nothing needs to give us courage. It's something we already have in plenty. Draw on your courage. Use it to be free.

We come to this life with two minds: the intellectual mind and the heart mind. You can determine which mind you're using by the presence, or absence, of doubt.

If there is any doubt, you are using your intellectual mind. No matter how difficult the choice in any given situation, the heart mind trusts the direction it takes, while the intellectual mind will usually be influenced by fears based on the dead past or the imagined future.

Invite change.

Accept change.

Celebrate change.

Life is a big party

and all you have to bring with you is…

…YOURSELF.

Are you willing to show up and celebrate?

To resist change is to resist Life.

Life is constant change.

Welcome it.

Sing.

Dance.

Play.

What do you mean you can't?

Don't let anything or anyone become more important than your happiness.

Simplicity.

Simplicity.

Simplicity.

What distractions does your mind use to keep you from committing to loving yourself?

That moment when you want to be wanted by someone else: that's the moment to go in. Do *you* want yourself, exactly the way *you* are?

The bottom line of any spiritual path is Love.

Love takes all the blinders and limitations off so that you can see the innocence in yourself and others.

To take full responsibility is to let go of ALL blame. That's a hard one. There is in the universe a Divine order, a perspective of perfection that is known only from Love. Only Love can produce the knowing that is so far beyond the mind's willingness to stretch.

There is only one truth.

Love is the truth.

     The <u>only</u> truth.

Anything that is not said from Love is a lie, often a very convincing lie, yet nevertheless a lie.

Fear and love are not the same thing.

They do not abide together.

Are you willing to welcome life's moment-to-moment opportunities, even if they are painful?

Choose love and you will learn the difference between pain and suffering.

Pain is an unavoidable part of life.

Suffering is a choice.

You have allowed your mind to be in control simply by believing what it tells you. The energy you put into supporting your mind's programs strengthens them, creating an abundance of fear that has you hooked.

Open your eyes and create an abundance of freedom. It's so simple that it sounds trite.

When you tell the truth, your mind wants to shut down on you.

Literally!

That's the extent of the power you've given the mind: to potentially make you sick. It can't do that without your permission.

You can even experience illness without *becoming* the illness.

Be the observer of your body.

When you're completely trusting the Holy Spirit of Love, there are no problems. Just an objective overview of what is going on in your world and the lives of the people around you.

Love will take you Home.

Home to that quiet, peaceful place of your creation.

Home to your innocence.

So many questions.

Only one answer.

Love.

How simple it is.

Sometimes the mind refuses to notice the extraordinary ways that love is not present in our relationships because it's frightening to think, "I'm living nose to nose with somebody and yet I am not close to them." You may have gotten so used to being joyless that you don't even recognize what I'm talking about.

You need love to get clarity,
not clarity to get love.

When you are willing to choose love,
clarity will follow.

Love fills all the nooks and crannies of your heart, giving the experience of being whole:

One with your body, mind, and spirit.

Love generates energy.

Fear creates fatigue.

Are you energized…or fatigued?

When you are choosing love, no one can take advantage of you. You are doing what your heart says, and you must do that no matter what. You are at the whims of no one.

Love has a chain reaction.

So does hate.

How quickly we are programmed to forget why we are alive in this life. We spend so much time looking for our purpose. It's so, so obvious. We're here to love. Too simple. We just <u>HAVE</u> to complicate it.

Simplicity.

Simplicity.

Simplicity.

The only way to see yourself clearly as who you truly are is to take off the glasses of society and see yourself through the eyes of Love.

Freedom is the reward for unconditional loving.

Living a loving life creates the experience of utter humility and extraordinary power.

Love

is the greatest treasure in life.

It keeps its promise.

It has no limits.

It is beyond forever…

…and even then.

Don't sit and wait for Love to happen. Love does *not* just happen. It's a choice.

Love is always available to us.

It is *not* an intruder. It waits to be invited.

It will serve you tirelessly without ceasing if you allow it to.

Giving is the heart of loving.

When people are in their minds, they often are afraid that they'll just give, give, give themselves away.

You can NEVER give yourself away. Love is an endless supply. It keeps regenerating itself.

Can you remember a time when you were feeling fullness, huge joy inside yourself with your heart desiring to be of use and service, happiness beyond your own understanding? Then, suddenly, a fear of being misunderstood or taken advantage of invades your peace, and you wonder what happened. 'Where did my peace go?'

It didn't *go*. You *left* it behind. When you surrender to fear, Love steps back, allowing you the space to experience your choice to fear. Yet it will remain right there, should you choose again to be who you really are: Love.

What you resist persists because you are struggling and fighting against it. The only way to win is to relax and let it be what it is. It is like the tide. Fight it if you will, although if you lie down and let it wash over you, it is going to go back out. I use my husband's passing as a touchstone of that kind of experience. Just see if you can resist death! The loss of a loved one is so painful that it feels like it is almost in your bones. You have to breath into it or suffer unimaginably. So I'm saying to you, the only way to have control in your life is to be with life as it is. That's when wisdom shows up and you will know exactly what to do for yourself to endure. Being afraid of death is such a drain. The "what is" is that you're *going* to die of something. You have a choice: resist the inevitable or die happy in surrender.

Love is the Spirit of who we are.

We could have peace in the world if everyone remembered that fact. And it *is* a fact.

The human mind creates a persona as it grows from childhood, and then it spends most of the human experience attempting to prove that, "This is who I am. I'm a person who…" Then it often spends the rest of its life doing its best to find the right spiritual modality to get back to the one truth:

Love is the Spirit of who we are.

My truth, your truth, his truth.

There is one truth…

Love.

You don't have to pretend anymore.

<u>You are Love</u>.

Relax.

Spiritually speaking, we are all nesters, wanting to nestle in and experience love.

Are you building your nest?

Are you willing to make your health, your spirit, and the health of your spirit come first? Will you put everything else second?

Myths abound, one being, "Ignorance is bliss."

Ignorance is simply ignorance,

the unwillingness to know.

Everyone seems to be going from pillar to post seeking enlightenment. Be still.

Enlightenment is seeking <u>YOU</u>.

Are you willing to let it find you?

What would your life look like if you did?

Willpower is <u>NOT</u> the same as willingness to be powerful.

Please get rid of the 'sort-of' and 'kind of' in your language. They only weaken every statement you make.

I sort of love you?

I kind of need a heart transplant?!

The fear of seeming arrogant keeps most people from expressing what they know with certainty. Hence, the watered-down language of 'kind of,' 'sort of,' 'maybe' that seems to protect the ego from rejection. Speaking and living the truth takes humility because it requires risking people's opinions. People will have their opinions no matter what you say or do.

The Good Opinion of Others = G.O.O.

Experience your own humility.

Give up the GOO.

Live big and bright and sure.

We will not change the world by who we elect as president. We will change it by who we are being in our own lives.

Who are you being?

Is it working for you?

When you are willing to alter a belief that creates a behavior that doesn't work and people notice it, you have made a difference in the world. People are so sure of who you will be that it's startling to see you do it differently. You'll capture their attention. When they see that you can change *because* you are willing to.

The following may be a very hard concept to embrace, especially since most of us are programmed from childhood to believe otherwise.

Stay with me. Here goes…

There is <u>NO</u> right or wrong. There are only one's models (based on programming) of what is right or wrong.

I jokingly say to my students that "right" is whatever "I" <u>want</u>.

"Wrong" is whatever "I" <u>don't</u> want.

However funny, it's also the way folks usually see life.

I want to trigger people's indignation. I want people to say, what does that mean? If you don't resonate with it, be with your questions or irritation and put the book down. See what shows up!

If you take yourself too seriously,

no one ever will.

Get rid of terms like fault. Fault takes on more responsibility than the situation calls for.

If you compartmentalize your life, you'll find living Love an impossible task. How do you live Love on the job, in the courtroom, at the bus station? Most people live Love at church or at the ashram or in other "appropriate" places. That makes their experience of Love inconsistent. They then question Love instead of their inconsistency.

Remember: There are no good addictions, not even the one to <u>not</u> having addictions.

Please join me in replacing *right* and *wrong* with *what works* and *what doesn't work*.

Love works.

Fear doesn't work.

We are so busy making rules and breaking them that we forget to simply trust Love.

If it is your belief that biological connections should maintain primary importance, then if your spouse has a conflict with your parent, and both make equal points, your allegiance must be with the parent. What a complicated web you've woven.

Life does not make common sense. It does make common lessons. If you insist that life make sense, you're bound to know great frustration.

We are here in this life to grow and become one, to tap into joy, and to be of selfless service. When you get that, life is exciting. When you don't get that, life is complicated.

Life isn't really complicated at all. No matter what's happening, it is what it is: *right on schedule*. Whether it's your schedule or not is something to look at.

We came here to play the game of life and then we start getting annoyed because it's not *our* game. We came here to play the game, *not* to take it over.

Life has its own way of being and when you know that and don't mind, then you can have fun. You just learn the one rule and play the best you can. And that one rule is to love yourself and each other and not mind whether it comes back.

Do you get that?

Patience is the key to winning the game of life.

How do you develop patience?

By accepting with grace the challenges that life provides.

What does it mean to accept with grace?

It means to relax into the breath.

Breathe deeply and say, "Yes."

The mind will resist, and you say, "Yes," and breathe again.

Be as loyal to the *yes* as your mind is to the *no*.

You win.

Language is the means of communication that we have, and so we use it to the best of our ability. However, it is often inadequate because life is a set of constant contradictions. Review everything I've written here. You'll see me contradicting myself left and right.

Just don't mind.

Life is full of contradictions. There will always be an exception to every rule.

So what!

Please don't torture yourself by wanting life to be fair or make sense!

Don't confuse yourself just because life is a grand contradiction. Learn not to mind and you'll be free.

Embrace the contradictions because that is how you win in the game of life. Be willing to surrender to the contradictions.

When you are choosing Love, you don't need commandments. This is what works in our home. This is what doesn't. Period.

Power addictions are always about fear. The greater the fear, the bigger the power trip.

Fear is like a sieve.

It doesn't hold water.

Love is a spiritual container that holds the
World.

Change requires change.

They say that the definition of insanity is to keep doing the same thing over and over again and think, "This time it's going to come out differently."

It's all about *doing* it differently.

Change. It's one decision away.

On the down side, no matter who you are, you are also one decision away from fear.

You can't be in two places at the same time.
You cannot be in love and fear simultaneously.

Don't be addicted to being a certain way. When you do that, you are making problems where there are none.

Fear puts an end to the <u>need</u> for understanding.

Will you dare to choose Love and compassion,

the doorway to understanding?

The grand contradiction is that life and love
cannot really be understood.

How can anyone truly make you do anything? When you believe that anyone can, there is always fear behind your rationale. Let go of the fear and you are free.

Fear is a <u>very</u> convincing liar.

Fear is a circle and so is Love.

Which do you want to dance in?

You are going to die at some point anyway.

Do you want to die in love?

Or do you want to die in fear?

Fear will keep you from donating anything: your body parts, your money, anything! What if I don't have enough? What if? What if? What if? The minute you hear your mind say, 'what if?' you are trapped because that's the imagined future usually based on the dead past. And right here and now, if you are dead, you are dead. And if that body part or organ can keep someone alive, why not?

It takes guts to live a spiritually focused life in a world where folks are programmed to believe, "We're only human."

Take time every day to create oneness with the All, and you will begin to know transformation.

Heart, mind, and spirit.

In order to be whole and complete (as well as happily fulfilled), the three must be united.

Think of your heart as the Love Center. Everyday take some time to address any unrest in your mind from that Love Center. Feel the peace that passes all understanding. When you allow your heart to be your guide, you'll feel the spirit of who you really are.

Want to create heaven on earth?

Create discipline.

Most people resist the word discipline because they define it as drudgery. Take this moment to see the word discipline with new eyes. See Love as a choice that you make again and again. What would your life look like if you created that 'discipline' of loving?

Most people don't believe that it is possible to be happy at all times. Happiness is not a state of being. It is a chosen practice.

Patience stems from compassion.

Your emotions are the children of your thoughts. They follow the lead of their parents. Be aware of your thoughts. Uplift them and the children, your feelings, will follow their lead.

No one is superior in consciousness. Some of us are more disciplined and are committed full on to the discipline of choosing love. Nonetheless, anyone can do it. And a beginner can be as conscious as someone who's been doing this for ten years just by creating that discipline.

If you believe in failure, know this:

Failure is not about falling down a thousand times; it's refusing to get up.

'Trying' is a word that will get you into trouble. You'll get kudos for 'trying' and it won't actually be getting you anywhere.

Steel has to be melted down before it can be made strongest. Respect the tempering process.

Stay away from the word 'boundary.' The minute you say it, it conjures up walls and resistance and separateness. You don't need that. Use the other 'b' word instead. 'Bridge.'

There are no discounts in the "Store" of

"Being Human."

You are required to pay full price.

Choose Love and it will be worth it.

Your body is the vehicle that transports the gift of Love in the world.

Keep the vehicle in top-notch working condition. Feed it with the best food you can afford. Rest it well. Treat it with tenderness and compassion.

Do this and you will be, by your example, responsible for having been the vehicle for transporting the most meaningful message in life: that to genuinely love others, you must start with yourself.

It's a lie to say, "I love you," to your husband when you hate your sister.

You cannot love and hate simultaneously.

Sorry.

If you are waiting for something to happen,

forget about it.

Nothing will.

Life is a creation.

It doesn't just happen.

Do not be confused by what you say is most important to you.

Watch what you do.

What you DO is what is most important to you.

Want to become more loving?

Speak to yourself in a way that is more loving.

Don't let your heart, which has the capacity for all the joy there is, take a backseat to your intellectual mind.

Instead of inviting people into our lives who want to join us in loving ourselves, we tend to invite people (especially romantic relationships) into our lives to further support the mind's *illusory* version of loving ourselves.

Stop now and please think about this with your heart.

The only way to keep your partner from never leaving you is to leave them first. Look and see if you may have already started suffocating them with your neediness.

Many books have been written programming people to believe that they are who and what they think.

Descartes said, "I think, therefore I am."

Please create an understanding of "I think, therefore I THINK."

You will not THINK your way to happiness. Letting go of thought is the roadmap to peace and joy.

This is a way of training your mind to be the servant of your heart. When your mind is trained to surrender to your heart, your mind will serve you in ways that make all your decision-making wiser.

Honor your mind simply as a glorious tool.

Don't let it be the boss of you.

The journey of being human has only two paths:

The path of love or the path of fear.

Which path have you been traveling? Which do you most often choose?

By now, you've figured out the path of love is the one on which you experience happiness.

Ask yourself now what story you use to take you off the path of love onto the path of fear. Then do yourself a favor—drop the story.

We feed our bodies at the very least three times a day. How reluctant we are to nourish our spirits three times a day.

Our concern for the spiritual body often taking a backseat to our care and obsession with the physical way we appear to others.

Do not mistake tolerance for compassion.

Today, pay attention to how often you hear yourself say that you are "trying" to accomplish something.

Things are not always what they appear to be.

Listen to your mind size up a person or a situation based on how things look.

Then, go deeper.

Past models and programming, the heart sees things exactly as they <u>are</u>, not as they seem to be. The heart observes and knows, free of judgment.

The proof?

The presence of your compassion.

Are you contributing to what you say you want? Is what you are doing a part of making this occur?

Life is constantly giving you clues that now is always the time to live your life.

A Universal Law:

If you are unhappy, you are not here.

What!!??

If you are unhappy, you are in your mind, running stories about the dead past or the imagined future.

Example: A person has been overweight during childhood. As an adult, the person is very conscientious about watching his or her weight. Steps on the scale this morning, notices a weight gain. The tendency then is to immediately create fear thoughts based on the unhappy childhood memories of peer abuse (dead past) then becoming fearful of being fat again (imagined future).

The message: Be here now.

If you let go of dead past and/or future fear, you'll be empowered to use your wits and energy to do what you can to lose your present weight gain and be peaceful and confident in the process.

So many make being present an itty-bitty part of why they are here on earth. The reason we are here on earth IS to be present.

Make your decisions NOW. You can't make a wrong decision.

Every decision takes you deeper into the place of learning.

Learn to trust life.

Learn to love yourself…

Allow yourself to be loved.

What more is there?

In this moment,

there is only this moment....

Are you in it?

Living your life now is not a suggestion. It is imperative. There is no other way to live.

Don't turn the page just yet.

Please sit now with this.

There's no right or wrong, just what serves and what doesn't. I have back issues. These are not problems. I work with it. I choose to see it as, " I have to sit closer to the edge of the chair tonight." And when I have really strong pain, I celebrate the fact that I can stand up and ease the pain or I can….There is always something I can do here and now. So stay present. Don't make your life challenges right or wrong.

Everything that shows up in your life is there
<u>for</u> you,

NOT against you.

Your future doesn't need attention. It is what you are willing to put into your here and now that will be the investment into your future.

NOW.

No Other Way.

No other place.

Here.

Now.

The only place you can really be is here. The only time you can actually experience is now. This moment.

Are you willing to know this, to own it right now in this moment, to step through all your resistance and claim your freedom? Stop reading right now. Close this book and experience the pure joy of simply being yourself.

Enlightenment is a moment-to-moment decision. Take the time right now to stop and ask yourself if you actually believe that one can be enlightened in this day and time.

Our minds are like computers.

Whatever program is in the computer will inevitably come out.

Just like the computer program, the mental program can be changed.

No matter how old the program, no matter how horrendous, it can be changed.

Are you willing to take responsibility for reprogramming?

Now?

Oneness starts here:

being one, whole and complete, in yourself.

There is no 'almost nearly' in surrender.

It either is or it ain't!

Nothing is ever what it seems, and, because of that, let whatever shows up simply serve Love. You can't do that unless you are surrendered to Love.

So let your focus be on SURRENDER.

Our minds so want us to believe that something or someone out there is partially responsible for the way we feel. Unfortunately and fortunately, we are 110% responsible for the way we react and make ourselves feel about anything.

You want a trustworthy relationship?

Then you've got to put all your trust into it.

All of it?

100%!!

Are you willing to get out of your mind, to let go of the details of why you are right? Are you willing to surrender your story, to stop making it more important than oneness, forgiveness, and love?

What-is is.

What does that mean, 'What-is is'?

It means that life is what it is and often there is nothing you can do about it. Resisting what-is is the road to suffering. You don't have to like what-is to accept it.

"How do I accept what-is if I don't like it?"

Practice saying 'yes' to what-is.

Take the deepest breath you can.

Exhale and say, 'Yes.'

'Yes.' 'Yes.' 'Yes.'…..

Practice.

'Yes.'

(Keep practicing.)

The minute you <u>allow</u> yourself to be out of control, you are <u>in</u> control.

What would your life be like if you accepted
and loved it exactly as it is?

Resistance does not work.

WHAT-IS JUST <u>IS</u>.

In acceptance there is peace.

In resistance there is pain and often suffering.

The choice is always ours.

It is just that simple.

(And no one ever said it was easy!)

What "Is" are you resisting in your life?

The only real common sense comes from a free spirit.

The rest is simply justification for addiction.

The only cause of unhappiness is resisting the "what is" of life.

It's pouring down rain on my birthday. Unhappiness isn't in the fact that it is raining. It is in the resistance to the rain. The rain on my birthday is the "what is." I surrender to the rain and find a way to enjoy my birthday, or I resist the rain and surrender to unhappiness.

Make sense?

Trust is a gift you give.

It is not earned or deserved.

Awareness is like a kitchen knife. It can be used to cut the bread or to kill. How do you want to utilize this powerful tool? Growing awareness must be coupled with love in order to be fruitful.

It is important to feel grief and to feel it fully.
If you stop short of feeling it fully,
you'll be stuck.

I'm going to explain to a man how you have twins and he's going to understand me? He's not going to understand me. He's going to say, "Thank God I'm a man." And that's the way it is and we have to get it. That's the beauty of the difference between men and women.

Happiness comes from honoring
the differences.

It's all about God. Like it or not. No matter how your mind resists, somewhere deep inside, you know, or you'd have put this book down by now.

So here it is:

God is with us when we're born into the human experience. God is with us when we release the human experience and return to our peace of origin (Spirit). Therefore, no need to fear life or death.

Be with that for a while.

God's rule, if you must call it a rule,

is to love one another.

<u>Simple</u>.

When you are connected to Love,

it's noticeable.

When you're not…

it's noticeable.

Timing is everything. God's timing is perfect. No matter what your mind thinks, nothing in your life occurs a second before its time or a second after.

The timing of it is perfect.

That's a tough one for the mind to accept.

God still has a sense of humor or we wouldn't still be roaming around this planet.

God sent us all here into the game we call life with a little magic potion for joyful living and said, "Drink it as soon as you get there," and we get so busy in the delivery room that we forget. As we get older and begin to experience unhappiness, we remember. "Wait a minute. I came with a magic potion. Now where did I put it?"

Life is the meditation.

If you have to go sit in a corner with your legs folded and your hands in your lap, you are limiting your experience.

I thank you so much for spending your precious time with me in the reading of this book. May you feel my spirit continuing to connect with yours as you move nearer and nearer to your heart's knowing.

May you claim the light of love that surrounds you.

If you'd like more information about Cinnamon's counsel, workshops, or her non-profit organization, Loving Life Foundation, or if you'd like to contact her directly with questions or comments, feel free to call her at 206.303.7602. You can also email her at cinnlofton@gmail.com.